LIFE LINES

MOTIVATING AND INSPIRING QUOTES - II

by

DR. MARCO WALDER

FOREWORD BY

CHAD SLAUGHTER

We O.W.N

P.O. Box 540861
Grand Prairie, TX 75054

www.marcowalder.com

Printed in the United States of America

Library of Congress Catalog Data: Walder, Marco

ISBN: 978-0-9854826-7-1 (sc)

This book is designed to provide information in regard to the subject matter. The author or publisher does not guarantee any benefits by the purchase or use of the material contained within. In an effort to be as accurate and complete as possible, please understand that errors may exist. Therefore, this publication should be used as a reference guide. The author or publisher assumes no liability or responsibility to any person or entity with regard to any loss, damage or any result alleged directly or indirectly to the information contained in this book.

FOREWORD

Life, as simple as the word sounds it is just as perplexing. We live in a world where our paths can have several forks and can take us on many incredible journeys. However, knowing the final destination of these journeys is increasingly difficult if not impossible. I was born the summer of 1978 in Dallas, TX to my mom who was a nurse and my father who was trucker driver. Both of which were hardworking people. However, my father also had a side hustle, drug dealing. What a mix right? Day in and day out I watched my mom work hard to keep my siblings and I on the right path.

Mom made sure that all of our necessities were taken care of while our father was out doing whatever. During those times life was hard and we had to grow up quick because mom was away at work trying to provide for us. Thank God for my older brother. My older brother Mike, taught me things that would become the foundation of who I am today. Things that only another man that you respected could teach you. Things like how to find jobs to keep money in your pocket and to utilize the skills you already have. Mike was the first entrepreneur that I met in my life. He showed me that you didn't have to do things the way everyone else did, but instead do them your way. My brother would go on to leave his job that he was well tenured at to pursue his own dreams of owning his own business. Most people would be scared to make that kind of move, but not my brother. This intrigued me. He would go on to owning his own car dealership and several other business ventures. After watching my brother all those years, he gave me the mindset that anything is possible with hard work and determination. That experience would provide one of the sparks for my life.

Having dreams and goals provide motivation for us to do the things we do on a daily basis. Every now and then we have to remind ourselves of how far we have come in our individual journeys. Our lives are made up of several pieces, moments, and experiences that all collectively make up our journeys. During my journey, I had the privilege to meet Dr. Marco Walder at a time where we both were at pivotal junctures in our young lives. Junctures that would not only solidify a friendship, but a brotherhood that has now surpassed twenty plus years. Dr. Walder reminds me of my brother. They have the same focus, drive, and entrepreneurial spirit. They would mirror each other from those aspects. They both did things unapologetically their way unknowingly motivating others along the way. I had the pleasure of watching Dr. Walder "grind" his way from a bachelor's degree to a doctoral degree. All of which took several years. From Dr. Walder, I learned that hard work and perseverance truly have to be powered by motivation. I have found that taking time to appreciate the seemingly small details is essential to my life and well-being. These details transpired during times in my life where I experienced and observed how transformation can occur by simple daily practices, such as reading daily inspirational quotes. Motivation can be either intrinsic or extrinsic and is proven to be a vital aspect of the human life experience. With more technology than ever before, distractions have more opportunities to derail us from our personal truths, consequently separating us from our sources of daily inspiration.

The journey of life, is the fuel for another installment of Dr. Marco Walder's series of inspirational books that are aimed at motivating individuals to embrace self-improvement practices for daily living. Dr. Walder has worked with people from diverse walks of life and he challenges us to live impactful lives on our own terms. Dr. Walder is the epitome of what perseverance, discipline and focus are. None of which could be executed without motivation and inspiration to make a difference. We must not allow ourselves to be consumed with the negativity, drama, and the standards of today's world we live in. Dr. Walder proves to us in this book that motivation is truly contagious. This book is envisioned to be a part of your day-to-day routine. Please allow these potent quotes to be impactful at the rise and sunset of your days. Dr. Walder you are an inspiration to us all. May God continue to bless you in all of your endeavors!!

Respectfully submitted,

Chadwick V. Slaughter
Former College All-American and NFL Football Player

Sometimes God has to get your attention and get you moving, by showing and making you feel that at any given moment, it all can be taken away from you at any given moment.

Often times in life we sit and become comfortable where we are. We put off dreams and goals that we can be working towards today, until tomorrow. Those goals may consist of going back to school, opening a business, or writing a book. Sometimes God has to "shake things up" to make you "wake up". God is a power who works in mysterious ways. Many times He has to get our attention by putting us in a situation that may be the worst, in order to get us "moving" so He can shift us into a better situation. Start today living your life because tomorrow is not promised and God is waiting.

What does this quote mean to you....

_____

_____

_____

_____

_____

_____

_____

_____

_____

_____

Only where there is consistency can there be accountability.

Attempting to hold someone accountable for expectations and desires in a non-structured environment will prove difficult to do. Consistency is something that can create habits, patterns, or even a way of doing things. When you have consistency you are able to implement rules and regulations or certain expectations that need to be adhered to on a daily basis. When consistency is not involved it makes holding someone accountable virtually impossible. Be consistent when it comes to displaying those behaviors and expectations you desire and then one can be held accountable.

What does this quote mean to you....

_____

_____

_____

_____

_____

_____

_____

_____

_____

_____

Many will want to enjoy your dreams, however very few will want to endure your nightmares.

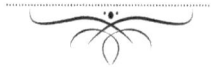

Ever notice some people only come around when you are on the "right side" of life? You ever ask yourself where were all of these fans and voices of praise and admiration when the sun was not shining so brightly on your life? Never forget, those who are truly for you will be by your side when you are on the right or the wrong side of life. Surround yourself with people of character and integrity and only then will you see the ones who are for you, no matter what. Always remember God will be there no matter what and through Him all things are possible.

What does this quote mean to you....

_____

_____

_____

_____

_____

_____

_____

_____

_____

_____

The great one seeks ways to solve the problem. The average one simply complains about it.

Problems will arise daily in your life no matter where you. You could be at work dealing with a deadline that seems impossible to meet. Or you could be having family problems that need your undivided attention. Either way complaining about the situation does nothing. However, working diligently to find a solution can often times create the necessary behaviors that will allow you to bring light to a dark situation. Change the way you think, view hard times, and difficult situations and positive results have the opportunity to follow.

What does this quote mean to you....

_____

_____

_____

_____

_____

_____

_____

_____

_____

_____

_____

Choosing to dive into a beautiful ocean is usually not the problem. Believing that you are mentally prepared and physically capable of swimming back out alive without knowing what is in the beautiful ocean usually is.

There may be nothing more beautiful than walking on the beach along side a beautiful ocean. The curiosity of what lies within that ocean can cause one to dive in without hesitation or to take there time until they are more comfortable with the waves and currents. Nevertheless, you only have one life to live and you only get one chance to do it. Many have coined the phrase, "living my best life" and each day that is exactly what you should do. Dive right into those dreams and goals you have set. Just make sure you are ready to deal with the high tides that may come your way before you do.

Reflection & Notes

What does this quote mean to you....

_____

_____

_____

_____

_____

_____

_____

_____

_____

_____

_____

Often times connections are not made because we focus more on why it cannot and should not happen instead of why it can and should happen.

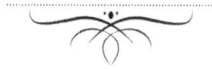

Many people in life find peace in creating mindsets that deter them from believing something is possible. They continuously find reasons to why success and greatness cannot happen in there life. These types of people will never enjoy the beauty of seeing God make what is believed to be impossible, possible. Work daily to create an uplifting mindset that helps you believe anything is possible and make those connections in life based on what can happen positively verses what can happen negatively. Do not allow fear to force you to make a decision that could hinder your opportunity at success.

What does this quote mean to you....

_____

_____

_____

_____

_____

_____

_____

_____

_____

_____

Often times the same people you thrive off talking about you yourself are emulating. Watch what you say because you could be talking about yourself.

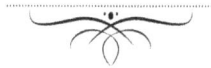

Being a walking contradiction is something many refuse to believe they are. Steady denouncing the actions and behaviors of others while displaying and living those same behaviors and actions daily. In life you will realize no one is perfect, not even you. Be slow to speak negatively on the behaviors and actions of another individual before taking the time to thoroughly evaluate your own. Many times the behaviors and actions you see have an underlying reason that could possibly shift the way you view a particular individual. Nevertheless, do not judge unless you to are ready to be judged as well.

What does this quote mean to you....

_____

_____

_____

_____

_____

_____

_____

_____

_____

_____

The true character of a person is revealed when it is time for them to help the next person. Many expect it, yet struggle to give it.

One of the "golden rules" in life is, "give and you shall receive" a powerful biblical scripture that lives deeply in the hearts of many. However, for a few these principals are not always deeply embedded. Many will ask you for assistance in various ways and these requests can seem unlimited. Now, when it is time for you to ask them for some assistance the request can often times go ignored or seemly unheard. Always remember God loves a cheerful giver and even when you give more than you receive, God sees and everything and your blessings for giving will to overflow.

What does this quote mean to you....

_____

_____

_____

_____

_____

_____

_____

_____

_____

_____

When you have the courage to let them see who you truly are then you will see if with you is where they really want to be.

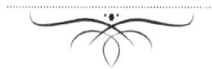

Being yourself is something many find difficult to do. Often times we attempt to win the prize by acting or behaving in a manner that does not truly represent who we really are. In life the best moments are when you can be transparent and vulnerable without being taking advantage of or judged. The representative you show someone is the representative you will have to continue to show them because the true individual may not be to their liking. However, if you start off from the beginning by showing them who you are, if they choose to stay, you know it is truly because of who you are.

24

What does this quote mean to you....

_____

_____

_____

_____

_____

_____

_____

_____

_____

_____

Some of the best moves in life that you will ever make involve being the first person to do what is necessary to help a situation deescalate.

Taking the first step to changing the result or outcome of a situation can ultimately start with you. However, the first step is often times the most difficult one to take. Pride, ego, and several other characteristics can often times prevent one from taking this first step. However, when one is able to evaluate a situation and see the good in taking that first step out weighs the bad, better days are in the near future. Today may be the day you mend a broken situation by simply having the courage to take the first step. Remember, change can ultimately start with you.

Reflection & Notes

What does this quote mean to you....

_____

_____

_____

_____

_____

_____

_____

_____

_____

_____

_____

Many people you encounter in life will have very little to offer so the choices and decisions they make reflect living a life with very little to lose.

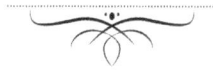

Each day will bring new encounters with new people. Many who will be total strangers and placed in your life for different purposes. Nevertheless, you have to take the time to learn each individual and seek the reason God has placed them in your life. Some of these people will have knowledge and power to offer you. Jewels and treasures of growth designed to enhance the person you are. Others will offer very little value which could in turn lead to them not valuing you. Remember, a person who has nothing to lose will often take chances and risks that do not add to others.

28

What does this quote mean to you....

_____

_____

_____

_____

_____

_____

_____

_____

_____

_____

As an educator if you do not take the time to learn and meet the child where they are you will never be able to build their trust to take them where you want them to grow.

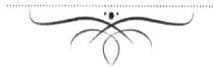

As an educator I have witnessed many students get left behind because they were not able to keep up with the class academically. The need to grow a child is one that starts with first, understanding where they are. By not understanding where a child is academically will prevent you from being able to teach them on their level. This disconnection will make it almost impossible to grow them. Impacting a child who needs your help to be the best they can be is a great feeling as an educator. Always remember, if you do not know you cannot do and the child will ultimately suffer.

Reflection & Notes

What does this quote mean to you....

_____

_____

_____

_____

_____

_____

_____

_____

_____

_____

You got to be careful because many of your "friends" really just want to keep seeing you be a crash dummy.

Often times those who are so called, "supporting us" really do not won't the best for us. Jealousy and envy can be in the hearts of those closest to you and every time you fail it gives them joy and happiness. Success can divide a family. It can destroy a friendship. It can even turn those who once loved each other against one another. Pay close attention to those who are applauding you and claim to be your friend because in the end they may actually turn out to be a foe. They may be a foe who thrives off seeing you fall and not grow.

What does this quote mean to you....

_____

_____

_____

_____

_____

_____

_____

_____

_____

_____

_____

Separation does not have to mean desperation. Many times it is the first step to elevation.

The first step to growing as a person often times means ridding yourself of unhealthy relationships. These relationships may come in the form of family members, friends, or even significant others. Surrounding yourself with energy that motivates you and inspires you to do more is what many need to keep going. However, many times we are afraid to put a relationship with an individual on hold because of how it may make them feel or how others may view us. If a person is not helping you move up then they are probably the one holding you down.

34

What does this quote mean to you....

_____

_____

_____

_____

_____

_____

_____

_____

_____

_____

_____

If they don't understand your dream they will never understand your sacrifices.

The hardest thing to do in life is help someone understand the things you have compromised and sacrificed to make your dreams come true. Often times many people see the finished product. Not the rough draft or hundreds of setbacks and failed attempts that have made you who you are today. Nevertheless, one who does not understand your purpose for your life and the dreams you ultimately want to attain will never be able to understand those tough sacrifices and compromises you make daily for them to come true.

What does this quote mean to you....

_____

_____

_____

_____

_____

_____

_____

_____

_____

_____

_____

Your actions won't always change ones behaviors and your behaviors won't always change ones actions.

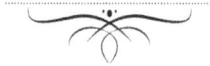

Changing what you do and who you are can work for you or against you. If you are changing because you want to be better and you are doing it for yourself then that brings about a positive result. However, if you are changing to make someone else happy you are taking a huge risk. Being who you are makes you unique. It gives you an identity no one else can claim. When you change to please someone else or to change the actions of another person the results may not turn out in your favor. In the end be who you are and if that does not work then they were not the one for you.

What does this quote mean to you....

_____

_____

_____

_____

_____

_____

_____

_____

_____

_____

The biggest changes can require the smallest of efforts.

Change, one word that can garner the attention of anyone. A word that can be filled with many actions that can challenge the heart and soul of an individual. Change, an action that must take place in your life if growth is desired. An action that often times requires the smallest of efforts, yet we avoid it for many reasons. Change can be good, it can be great, however change can also be hard-work. Change can push you to limits that one may not be comfortable with. More than anything change depends on your efforts. Nevertheless, if you desire a different result in your life change is inevitable.

What does this quote mean to you....

_____

_____

_____

_____

_____

_____

_____

_____

_____

_____

_____

You cannot see a good thing with bad vision.

Past experiences can often times cloud your vision or provide a polluted perspective of something or someone that could possibly be good for you. Having a clear mind and giving each opportunity a fair chance can prove difficult for someone who has experienced a life of hurt and pain. Nevertheless, one must work to heal from those experiences in order to see the good in others. Often times we allow those past experiences to dictate how we will deal with new situations that are presented to us in our lives, and is that honestly giving each situation and yourself a fair chance? No!

Reflection & Notes

What does this quote mean to you....

_____

_____

_____

_____

_____

_____

_____

_____

_____

_____

If you do not change the climate of the culture you risk killing the effectiveness of new strategies.

Many leaders dive into new situations and leadership roles with the mindset of implementation. Yet, they do not start with the mindset of cultivation. A good leader knows that in order for new strategies to be successfully implemented they must first get the employee's to "buy in". This aspect is created by changing the culture, the mindsets, and the negative behaviors that currently exist. A difficult task to say the least, yet a necessary one if success is desired. It takes time and often times in order to change the climate one has to remove some of the old and bring in more of the new.

Reflection & Notes

What does this quote mean to you....

_____

_____

_____

_____

_____

_____

_____

_____

_____

_____

As you work to be better you may find yourself becoming different. As you become different do not be afraid to walk alone and be comfortable enough to stand away from the crowd.

There is an old rap song with the lyrics, "walk this way, talk this way" and in life you may just find yourself walking in a different way, along a different path. This path could very well have you talking in a certain way. A certain way that allows you to grow. A way that propels you to distance yourself from those who may not be aligned with the person you are working to become. This choice could cause you to stand away from the crowd which ultimately means you may begin to stand out. Have the courage to create your own path and follow it to your destiny.

What does this quote mean to you....

_____

_____

_____

_____

_____

_____

_____

_____

_____

_____

You cannot keep reading the same book and expect a different ending. Nothing changes until you do.

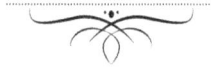

Waking up every day with the expectations of something new to be on your horizon is a great thing. However, this is something you may never see if you keep doing the same things that are not helping you to reach new heights. Goals are not reached by repeating the same bad habits every day. Obstacles are not overcome by approaching them in the same unsuccessful way. Nevertheless, if you truly want to see that change you desire focus on turning those bad habits into good ones. Focus on approaching those difficult obstacles in a new more effective way and your ending will be different.

What does this quote mean to you....

_____

_____

_____

_____

_____

_____

_____

_____

_____

_____

Do not judge the shoes of someone else because if you had to walk in them it may be more than you can handle.

Observing the life of someone else may lead you to pass judgment onto them based on the current situation that you see them in. However, we have to be careful when we decide to judge the life of another. Many people are going through situations and dealing with the ups and downs of life that many of us could not imagine dealing with. Always remember do not judge when you see someone looking as if life is getting the best of them, or you assume they are currently on the rough side of life. Instead take the time to give thanks because your situation, good or bad, could always be worse.

50

Reflection & Notes

What does this quote mean to you....

_____

_____

_____

_____

_____

_____

_____

_____

_____

_____

The one who really wants you in their "big picture", understands the value and importance of simply being consistent with doing those things that create the "little pictures".

In life those "little things", help to build momentum towards those "big things". Being consistent is something that can go a long way with an individual. Showing someone a consistent level of interest can prove those first words you shared with them are actually valid. This can also build a sense of trust and dependability. It helps a person believe that if they decide to share their life with you they can depend on you. In the work place this shows your employer or your employees that you have a high standard of professionalism and a great work ethic which is valuable.

What does this quote mean to you....

_____

_____

_____

_____

_____

_____

_____

_____

_____

_____

Many love to join the winning team once you have made it to the top, however very few are willing to go through what it takes with you before you get there.

When times are rough your true friends and family members who are by your side, no matter what, will be revealed. During these times you learn a lot about yourself and you also learn a lot about others. Similar to a bandwagon fan, everyone loves to scream the winning teams name. However, when the same team begins to lose and have a few down years many of those fans tend to disappear. Always be aware of those individuals who seem to only appear when you are on the smoother side of the mountain. Those are the ones you do not need.

What does this quote mean to you....

_____

_____

_____

_____

_____

_____

_____

_____

_____

_____

_____

MW

Potential, ambition, and drive will never be enough for a person who is looking for a "finished product".

These characteristics will never be enough for a person who is always looking for someone to be totally complete in all areas of life. Taking a chance on someone who is obviously still growing in a certain aspect of their life takes a high level of maturity. This can require many sacrifices, compromises, and unselfish practices they are not willing to commit to. It is also a great sign for the one who is transparent and still growing because it shows that this individual is not the one for you. Also this supports no need to waste any time on them because they are not willing to invest the time in you.

Reflection & Notes

What does this quote mean to you....

_____

_____

_____

_____

_____

_____

_____

_____

_____

_____

If they cannot stand with you at the bottom and support your grind, leave them where they stand and keep pushing towards the top.

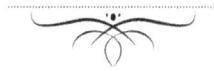

Support is something many speak about giving, yet very few are actually seen doing. Support can be a vital element in making dreams come true. We all need supportive people in our life to encourage us to "keep pushing" and to "keep fighting". Those people in our corners to uplift and motivate us when times get hard and the pressures of life seem unbearable. More than anything, we need those individuals in our lives that will keep us focused with the "never quit and never settle" attitude. Nevertheless, support can come and go so be sure to have ways to keep yourself going as well

58

What does this quote mean to you....

_____

_____

_____

_____

_____

_____

_____

_____

_____

_____

You better learn to toot your own horn because many times that may be the only music you hear.

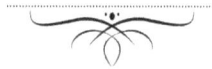

One thing about the journey to the top, it can certainly become a lonely one. Looking from external praise can be something you may not often receive. When those times come you must be able to look deep inside yourself and find a reason to simply, "celebrate you". Finding ways to rejoice in small accomplishments keeps you going as you pursue much bigger ones. If you are always depending on someone else to toot your horn you could easily find yourself in a state of depression and giving birth to a feeling of failure. These feelings are not ones to live with so learn to celebrate you!

What does this quote mean to you....

_____

_____

_____

_____

_____

_____

_____

_____

_____

_____

The beauty of learning how to "effectively listen" allows you to really hear what you need to know.

Listening is an art, it is a skill. Learning how to listen effectively takes times and patience. Many people listen, however they do not listen to understand. Most only listen so that in return they have a chance to be understood. When you are able to train your ear to listen at a high level you are able to digest and process vital information in order to make more sound decisions. Being able to make more sound decisions could possibly prevent you from ending up in a bad situation. By listening effectively you may also avoid wasting valuable time on people who do not deserve it.

Reflection & Notes

What does this quote mean to you....

_____

_____

_____

_____

_____

_____

_____

_____

_____

_____

MW

You cannot go to a fishing hole looking to come back with milk.

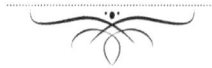

Putting yourself in the right position to achieve a goal first starts with ensuring you are aligned with the necessary requirements needed to reach the desired goal. This means planning with the end in mind so you are able to monitor and evaluate each move you make effectively. While monitoring and evaluating your moves you are providing yourself with the opportunity to make adjustments if needed. This will keep you on the right path that ultimately leads to reaching your goal. If you go after a dream with a different end in mind do not be surprised when your dream does not come true.

What does this quote mean to you....

_____

_____

_____

_____

_____

_____

_____

_____

_____

_____

It is hard to turn a broke dream into a rich reality.

We all have dreams and goals that we want to bring to life. However, many of those dreams and goals require money in order for us to pursue it. Often times, this money comes from a family member or an investor. Take the time to create a "blue print" of your dream. This is also known as a "business plan". With this business plan you can present your dream and goals to a potential investor who may support and provide you with the necessary funding which will allow you to bring something you are passionate about to life. Remember, help often comes when it is properly asked for.

66

What does this quote mean to you....

_____

_____

_____

_____

_____

_____

_____

_____

_____

_____

_____

Just because you walked away and got out of a "bad situation" does not necessarily mean you are putting yourself in a better situation.

The struggle can definitely get the best of us during a trying time in our lives. Maybe it is a relationship that is going south or maybe you are going to a job day after day that is just not the job for you. Before you exit stage left or abandon the situation, remember, God is the creator of good and bad. He also promised us that He will never put more on us than we can bare. This could be a time He is using to develop a characteristic in you that is lacking. So before you move yourself be patient and sit still. Never forget, God does his best work in the midst of the storm, not after.

What does this quote mean to you....

_____

_____

_____

_____

_____

_____

_____

_____

_____

_____

Having capital gives you a great opportunity to capitalize.

Money, Money, Money.......... Money!!... Money!!.. Needless to say I have emphasized the word, "money" for several reasons. When one is financially blessed it makes life somewhat easier in a way. Yes, problems will still arise and the struggles of life will still exist, however those problems and struggles will definitely be different. When you are wealthy you have money to take big risks. Whether these risks involve investing in a new venture or just simply being able to take advantage of a special deal having accessible funds can make a huge difference in your life.

What does this quote mean to you....

_____

_____

_____

_____

_____

_____

_____

_____

_____

_____

Sometimes it's good to take what medicine is being fed to you, digest it, and let it help cure you instead of throwing it back up in the other direction just because it's a hard pill to swallow.

Constructive criticism, the truth, unwanted feedback whatever you choose to call it, allow it to mold and cultivate you in a positive way. Often times we seek those terms from people who we believe care about us and have our best interest in mind. However, do we honestly allow those words to pierce our hearts and enter our souls? Or do we put a wall of reject and rebel against those perceptions and opinions that may not be the ones we desire to hear. Either way learn to take the good with the bad and use both sides of the coin to help you develop and grow.

72

What does this quote mean to you....

_____

_____

_____

_____

_____

_____

_____

_____

_____

_____

When the hunger for success will not let you sleep, get up and grind because you have goals to reach.

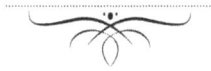

When the pursuit of a dream or a goal is birthed within you and the passion for achieving this dream or goal is at an uncontrollable level, nothing will stop you from bringing it to life. Not even the need for one of the most important components needed in life, sleep. Sleep to a dream catcher is often times a rare commodity. Something they do not get a lot of, however when that dream or goal is finally reached and you are able to look back on those early mornings and sleepless nights it makes you appreciate all of the hard-work and sacrifices you made throughout the process.

What does this quote mean to you....

_____

_____

_____

_____

_____

_____

_____

_____

_____

_____

Often times you can look at a person before saying one word to them and realize the juice will not be worth the squeeze.

A great gift that God gives us is the ability to use our past situations to shape how we see the present and how we will go forward in the future. One of those great gifts is the ability to have discernment. Often times the discernment you have for a situation will prevent you from taking a step that could possibly place you in a bad situation. This same discernment allows you to see a person and simply observe their body language and allow the lack of energy to give you a preview that nothing good will come from dealing with them. Nevertheless, still stay neutral and give a fair chance.

What does this quote mean to you....

_____

_____

_____

_____

_____

_____

_____

_____

_____

_____

_____

Life has shown us even the strong get weak.

Life is day to day roller-coaster that takes us up and brings us down. Nevertheless, many people spend a majority of their days uplifting, inspiring, and motivating others to keep going and to never give up. However, who is there to motivate the motivator, to inspire the inspirer, to uplift the uplifter? Often times they are left to fend for themselves. They are forced to show a strength that may not always be there. Do not forget to check on those who you think can handle it all because even they could be at the edge of life ready to jump in order to get away from it all.

What does this quote mean to you....

_____

_____

_____

_____

_____

_____

_____

_____

_____

_____

Many people cannot move forward in life because their attitude and mindset still suffers from a failed and hurtful past.

Do you have a family member, friend, or co-worker who seems to always be stuck in the past? A past that hurt them in several ways or put them in a bad situation in life that they just for some reason cannot get over? In addition, no matter how much support and loving advice you share with them nothing seems to give them the desire to move on with their life. These people are stuck and often times no matter what you do it will never be enough. The longer you stay around them the more they will drag you down with them because they will not emotionally move on until they are ready to.

What does this quote mean to you....

_____

_____

_____

_____

_____

_____

_____

_____

_____

_____

Sometimes you just want to tell someone to turn that light that is supposedly waiting for you at the end of the tunnel, the hell off and let's pack it up and go home.

No one ever said chasing dreams and goals was going to be easy. Often times, they can be quite challenging. They can be grueling, tiresome, stressful, and overwhelming. Sometimes you reach a point in your life where you just want to give up and quit. It is at this point you must dig deep and find your "why" for having that dream or those goals. Let your why or even your "why not" keep you upright and pushing towards success. It has been said anything worth having is worth going the extra mile for and a dream or a goal that will make your life better is definitely worth it.

What does this quote mean to you....

_____

_____

_____

_____

_____

_____

_____

_____

_____

_____

When a person you are conversing with does not strive to understand, you will always be misunderstood.

Communication, something many feel they are great at, yet lack the skills necessary to truly be effective. When you are trying to communicate with a person who is not an effective listener you will often times be misunderstood. Being an effective listener is a skill that requires an individual to be patient, open minded, and desiring to reach a common ground with you before the tense conversation even begins. The person who learns how to effectively communicate will be able to understand and keep the main focus of a conversation the main focus.

What does this quote mean to you....

_____

_____

_____

_____

_____

_____

_____

_____

_____

_____

Stop allowing your expectations for another to overly exceed your own reality.

When you put unrealistic expectations on an individual that you, yourself cannot live up to it can ultimately set you up for failure. These unrealistic expectations can also set you up for major disappointments. Disappointments that will continue to haunt you until you allow your expectations to align with your own reality. Simply ask yourself, "how can I ask this of a person and I myself am not capable of providing it myself". This simple question can save you from having failed connections. If you do not change this mindset you will find yourself asking for more than you can even offer.

What does this quote mean to you....

_____

_____

_____

_____

_____

_____

_____

_____

_____

_____

The situation in your life had to look impossible for you to understand that God was the real MVP who brought you through it, otherwise you would of thought you did it.

Many times when we overcome a difficult situation or pull through a rough patch in our lives we tend to believe we were the ones who got us through it. In actuality God was the one who helped us through each and every situation that we have overcame in our lives. When the sun shines He is by our side and when the rain comes He remains by our side. Never forget He is the maker and creator of all and nothing is possible without God overseeing it. During those impossible times that ultimately become possible times, He is the reason for you overcoming a rough season.

What does this quote mean to you....

Before you have that conversation about love, you better have that conversation about money.

All is fair when we are in love and have a lot of money, right? It amazes me how relationships can start out on a high note and once a financial hardship occurs the relationship suddenly falls apart. The love that was once the key element to the union has now become a lost affection with no GPS love locater. Nevertheless, before you fall head over heels for someone make sure you are transparent about where you are in life, in all areas, including financially. Be honest and stay within your financial comfort zone when getting to know someone. Love should not be something you have to buy.

What does this quote mean to you....

_____

_____

_____

_____

_____

_____

_____

_____

_____

_____

Do not allow a thief of negativity to steal your positive treasures of peace.

Many times in life you will have a knock at your door, a text message early in the morning, a phone call late at night, and on the other end will be someone seeking to bring you out of your comfort zone of peace. Seeking to take from you something that you work daily at protecting. Believing they have the power to get you to engage in something that will bring out the negative side in you. These people are "peace thieves" and it is up to you to protect your peace by any means necessary. Always remember no one can enter your peace vault unless you give them the combination to do so.

What does this quote mean to you....

_____

_____

_____

_____

_____

_____

_____

_____

_____

Stop being anxious for the nothing and learn to be patient for the something.

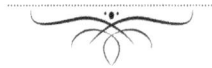

Patience is something that comes with maturity. It is a skill that very few truly master. However, when you learn to be patience for something instead of anxious for nothing great things will happen in your life. Often times we see something and instantly get excited because of how it looks and what we potentially believe it could possibly be. Whereas the wise one maintains their emotions and allows their patience to reveal the true value of those things our eyes can fool us into giving false value too. The old saying still lives, "everything that glitters is not gold".

What does this quote mean to you....

Always remember just because they are smiling with you does not mean they are cheering for you.

Many of those who are close to you find happiness in seeing you fail. However, they will pretend as if they are sharing the same emotions when failure strikes. Nevertheless, you will discover many people take pleasure in watching you come in last place. These people will talk behind your back, not support your endeavors, and often times cheer heartlessly for you to continue to fail. Through it all keep your circle small and those who are truly loyal to you close. Watch those who give you false cheers of support and allow those gestures to fuel your journey towards success.

Reflection & Notes

What does this quote mean to you....

_____

_____

_____

_____

_____

_____

_____

_____

_____

_____

Advice should be delivered like a UPS package, intact and carefully placed on their door step then maybe the advice will be received in the same manner.

Advice, something we get a lot of from various people we encounter in our lives. Often times we only accept advice from those we trust, love, and consider to have our best interest at heart. Nevertheless, many tend to forget, "how" you say something can mean just as much as, "what" you say. Being tactful with your words shows a level of care and respect. It also shows that the person who is giving the advice cares about you and how you feel. Remember, take your time and choose your words wisely because you would want someone to do the same for you.

98

What does this quote mean to you....

_____

_____

_____

_____

_____

_____

_____

_____

_____

_____

Only speak into existence those things in life you want to experience.

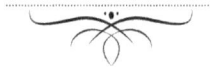

Often times in life we can talk ourselves into bad situations and out of taking a chance on a possible good one. Power lies in your words. This is also a biblical reference in which God speaks to how your tongue can either give life or cause death. Nevertheless, speak positive words over your life. This will give you a positive mindset and create more positive outlooks. Whatever you speak into the world be prepared to possibly receive it good or bad. God hears all and you want Him to hear more of those positive things you desire in your life verses the negative ones.

What does this quote mean to you....

_____

_____

_____

_____

_____

_____

_____

_____

_____

_____

MW

The difference between, "time wasted" and "wasted time" is you chose to do one and you were invited to do the other.

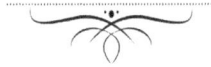

One thing in life you cannot get back is time. Time is something very valuable to many of us and the last thing we desire is for someone to waste it. Many times we waste our own time by not being productive, procrastinating, or by not taking advantage of the golden moment. Then you have those situations where others waste your time by not living up to who they sold to you they were. Or by simply playing games and taking you on journey's that lead to nowhere. Either way you cannot get your time back so use your timely wisely.

What does this quote mean to you....

_____

_____

_____

_____

_____

_____

_____

_____

_____

_____

If you are tired of receiving a lot of "no's" in life maybe you need to stop giving so many out.

Hearing the word, "no" can do several things to a person. It can cause depression, bring on a feeling or failure, or bring about a sense of accomplishment in the midst of temptation. However, if you are always the person saying "no" to helping others, do not be surprised when those same "no's" are reflected back at you. It is still true, the more you give the more you will receive. Nothing adds more value to your life like giving and helping others in need. So the next time you prepare yourself to say, "no" remember this could be God's way of setting you up to receive a "yes" in the near future.

What does this quote mean to you....

Greatness is a gift that has to be nurtured like a fine wine.

Becoming a student of your craft is a great way to become a master of your gift. Your gift should only get better with time. This only happens through trial and error. Allow failure to become a jewel and each time you fail allow it to be a learning experience. The more you learn the more you will grow. By studying, researching, and watching others who are blessed with your same gift is an awesome way to add new techniques and strategies to your craft that can possibly advance you to the next level. This advancement of your gift may also add financial gains.

What does this quote mean to you....

_____

_____

_____

_____

_____

_____

_____

_____

_____

_____

You cannot go swimming and expect not to get wet.

Every risk you take in life guarantees two things, you will either fail or succeed. There is no way around these two outcomes. However, understand that if you commit to doing something an outcome will be the result. Now whether the outcome is one you are prepared to accept, embrace, and live with is another thing. Do not think you can put yourself in a compromising situation and not experience the consequences that could possibly come with that decision. As one desires to enjoy the positive outcomes you must be willing to embrace the negative ones.

What does this quote mean to you....

_____

_____

_____

_____

_____

_____

_____

_____

_____

When you are going through hell search deep to find something that feels like heaven to hold on too, to get you through.

Life has a funny way of kicking you while you are down. It can also be unforgiving and heartless. All in all, life can and will take us to a place that we feel is the lowest we have ever been on this earth. Nevertheless, during those times look inside yourself and find those hidden jewels and priceless treasures that have gotten you to the place you are as a person and allow those highs to keep you motivated and inspired while going through life's lows. More than anything continue to seek God in the midst of the storm and remember tough times do not last forever.

What does this quote mean to you....

_____

_____

_____

_____

_____

_____

_____

_____

_____

_____

_____

One may never understand the power of forgiveness until they are the one's asking for it.

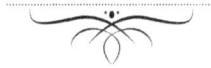

Ever have a friend or a family member listen to a situation you were in and tell you to crucify the person? Or maybe you made a mistake and you are trying to own up to it and the person you are owning up too, just is not accepting your apology. Do not allow this the stop you from doing what you feel you need to do in order to forgive yourself. Often times we apologize to others hoping they will forgive us and they do not and will not. At this moment take your words of regret and allow them to bring peace within you. Also, learn to forgive because one day you too will be seeking forgiveness.

What does this quote mean to you....

_____

_____

_____

_____

_____

_____

_____

_____

_____

ABOUT

Dr. Marco Walder is an educator, author, and speaker. A native of Dallas, Texas, Marco earned a Bachelor of Science degree in Interdisciplinary Studies and a Master of Education in Secondary Education from Alcorn State University. He also earned his Doctor of Education in Sport Management from Northcentral University and plans to be an advocate for improving the academic performance and higher education graduation rates of urban student-athletes.

During his undergraduate matriculation, he was four year letter winning football player. Dr. Walder is a member of Phi Beta Sigma Fraternity, Incorporated and is an active member in his local community. Dr. Walder is also a member of Kappa Delta Pi, an international honor society for higher education graduates who achieved high academic standards during their doctoral pursuit. Dr. Walder is a strong Christian and roots his message in a biblical foundation. He attends Concord Church under the leadership of Pastor Bryan Carter.

A noted speaker, Dr. Walder has presented for Dallas Independent School District, the El Centro Community College TRIO program, the Brookhaven Community College Black History Month Expo, and at local schools including Maynard Jackson Middle School and Oliver Wendell Holmes. He has also ventured outside the state to various cities such as Lake Charles, LA and Gulfport, MS to share his positive and uplifting messages.

www.ingramcontent.com/pod-product-compliance
Lightning Source LLC
Chambersburg PA
CBHW031558040426
42452CB00006B/345